Timeless Tiles in Latch Hook

Latch hooking is an easy technique that involves using a latch hook tool to knot pieces of yarn onto latch hook canvas to create unique art and home décor. *Timeless Tiles in Latch Hook* provides you with four interesting and enduring designs that you can use throughout your home in a number of ways! Once your tiles are completed, you can use them as wall hangings or even turn them into stunning pillows. Our detailed instructions, complete with color charts and helpful diagrams, will walk you through each step of completing these tiles. The possibilities are endless! Get started revamping your home décor with these timeless tiles today.

LEISURE ARTS, INC. • Maumelle, Arkansas

Timeless Tiles

SHOPPING LIST

***Note:** If using precut yarn strands, you will need additional yardage to match the yarn around the outer edge of the project for finishing the edges. If using yarn from a skein, additional yardage is included for finishing the edges.*

- ☐ four 20" x 20" (50.8 cm x 50.8 cm) pieces of 3.75 mesh (4 stitches per inch) latch hook rug canvas
- ☐ latch hook tool
- ☐ 4-ply rug yarn:
  - dark red — approximately 3100 2½" (6 cm) precut yarn strands + 5 yards (4.6 m) to finish outer edges **OR** 220 yards (201.2 m)
  - dark blue — approximately 2800 2½" (6 cm) precut yarn strands + 5 yards (4.6 m) to finish outer edges **OR** 200 yards (182.9 m)
  - medium blue — approximately 2600 2½" (6 cm) precut yarn strands + 5 yards (4.6 m) to finish outer edges **OR** 186 yards (170.1 m)
  - tan — approximately 3000 2½" (6 cm) precut yarn strands + 5 yards (4.6 m) to finish outer edges **OR** 213 yards (194.8 m) 0
  - light blue — approximately 1600 2½" (6 cm) precut yarn strands **OR** 116 yards (106.1 m)
  - copper — approximately 2200 2½" (6 cm) precut yarn strands **OR** 158 yards (144.5 m)
  - light gray — approximately 1600 2½" (6 cm) precut yarn strands **OR** 116 yards (106.1 m)
- ☐ 1¼" x 3" (3.2 cm x 7.6 cm) piece of cardboard (if cutting your own yarn strands)
- ☐ four 16" x 16" (40.6 cm x 40.6 cm) pieces of felt for backing
- ☐ craft glue for attaching backing
- ☐ tapestry (yarn) needle
- ☐ scissors
- ☐ masking tape
- ☐ safety pins
- ☐ permanent marker (optional)
- ☐ sewing clips or clothespins (optional)

Instructions

Read the **General Instructions**, page 14, and familiarize yourself with the charts.

1. Use masking tape to cover edges of each canvas square to prevent fraying.
2. If cutting your own yarn, refer to **Cutting Your Own Yarn Strands**, page 16.
3. Separate the yarn colors so that it's easy to pick up the correct color as you work.
4. Lay out your canvas, ensuring it is facing the correct direction (see **Latch Hook Canvas**, page 14).
5. Refer to **How to Latch Hook**, page 17, to knot the design.
6. Remove the masking tape and trim the excess canvas 1½" from the latch hook area on all sides.
7. Refer to **Making A Wall Hanging**, page 18, to complete four wall hangings.
8. Refer to **Trimming**, page 19, to trim your project.
9. Refer to **Hanging Your Wall Hanging**, page 19, to hang your wall hangings.

Safi

light grey	light blue
tan	blue
copper	dark blue
dark red	

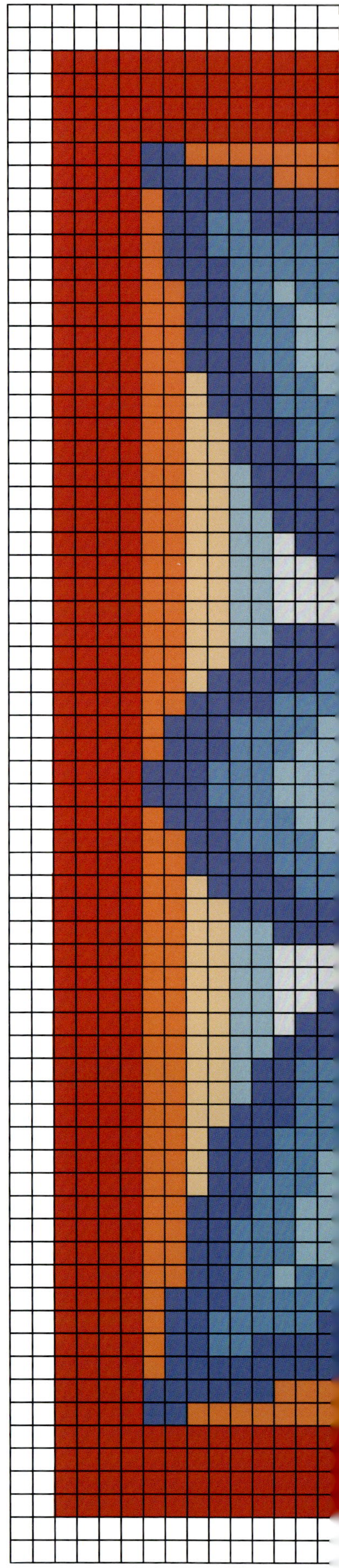

Gray area indicates last row of previous section of design.

Gray area indicates last row of previous section of design.

Tangier

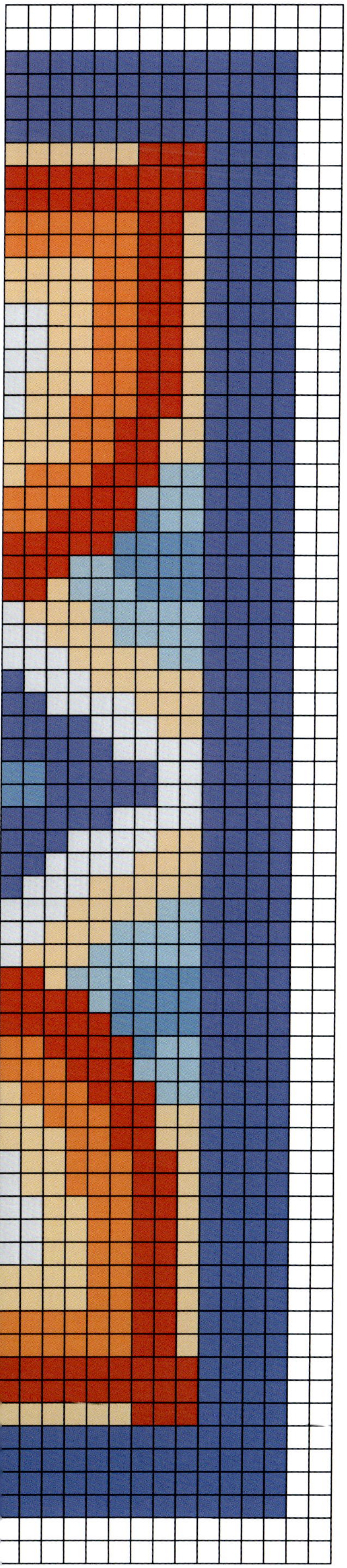

- light grey
- tan
- copper
- dark red
- light blue
- blue
- dark blue

Casablanca

- light grey
- tan
- copper
- dark red
- light blue
- blue
- dark blue

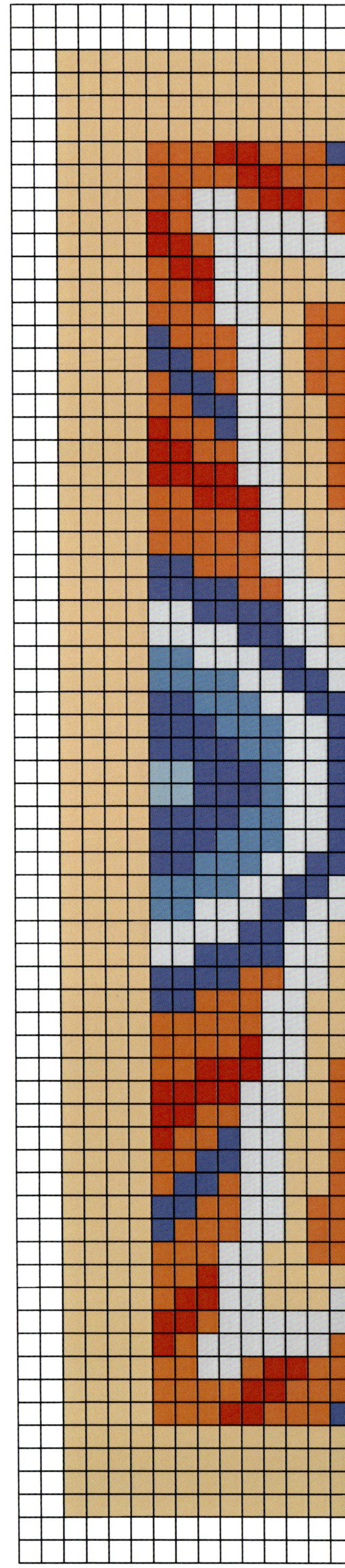

Gray area indicates last row of previous section of design.

Gray area indicates last row of previous section of design.

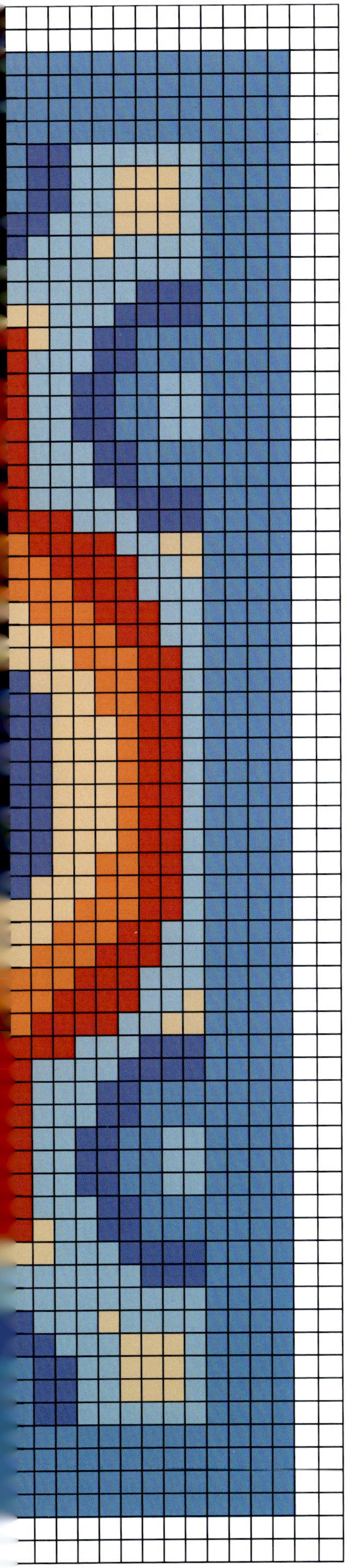

- light grey
- tan
- copper
- dark red
- light blue
- blue
- dark blue

Create an eye-catching accent pillow by simply hand stitching your completed latch hook tile to a pre-made or purchased pillow! This technique is easy enough that you'll want to give all your existing pillows a face lift!

LATCH HOOK CANVAS

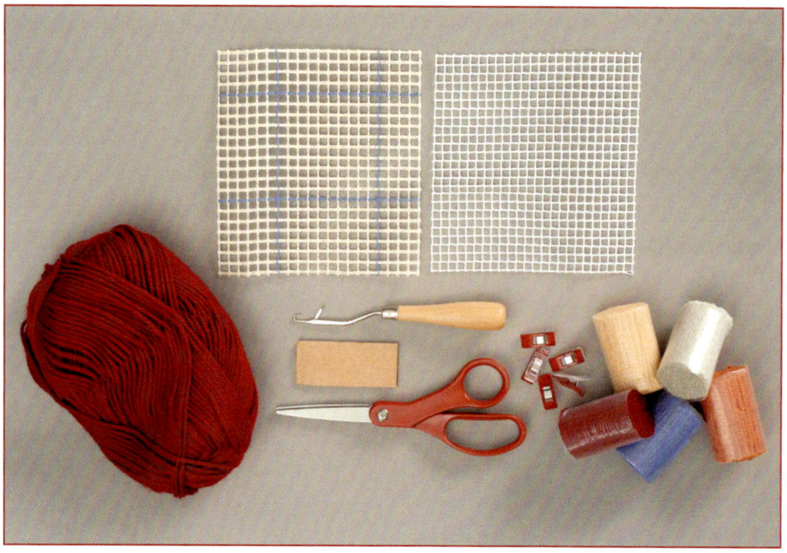

Latch hook canvas is made up of a sturdy woven grid of threads that you can loop folded yarn strands onto as indicated on a chart, forming a design. The canvas is woven with two strands of thread vertically and two strands horizontally. The horizontal strands run parallel to each other. The vertical strands are twisted around each other and intersect with the horizontal strands ***(Fig. 1)***. Your knot will be worked around a pair of horizontal strands. The twisted, vertical strands add strength to the canvas and will be left bare. Some latch hook canvas simply comes in white. Some latch hook canvas comes with every tenth vertical and horizontal strand woven in another color ***(Fig. 2)***. This helps when counting squares.

Fig. 1

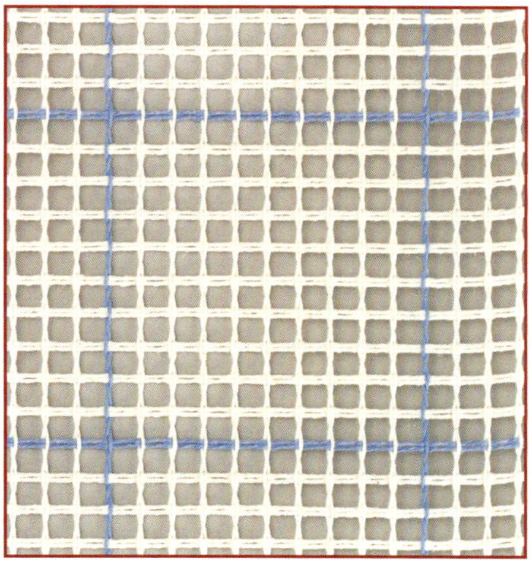

Fig. 2

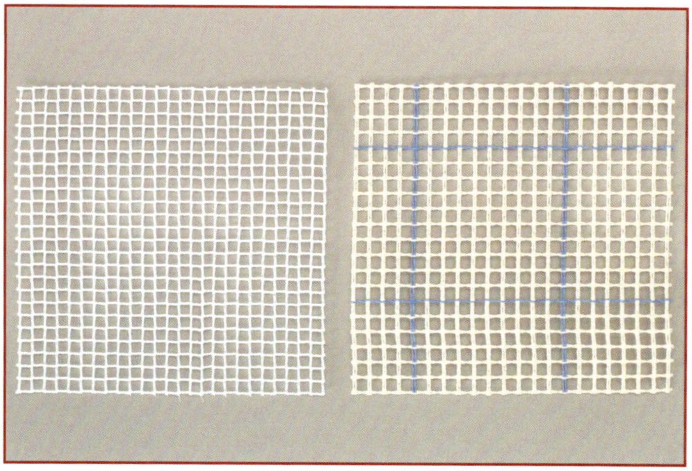

Latch hook canvas comes in a variety of mesh sizes. This project uses 3.75 mesh canvas. This will yield 4 squares per inch. The measurements given in the Shopping List allows for 2" of excess unworked canvas beyond the outside edges of the design.

YARN

This project is worked with 2½" (or 6 cm) yarn strands. After knotting the yarn strand around the horizontal strands of the canvas, this will make the pile length (how tall the yarn ends will be when the rug is laid flat) approximately 1". The Shopping List includes an approximate number of 2½" strands needed for each color of yarn used plus the yardage needed to finish the outer edges. You can use precut 2½" strands or you may choose to cut the strands yourself from skeins of yarn in order to find the color you desire.

Using Precut Yarn Bundles

Precut yarn strands are typically sold in bundles. The number of strands given in each bundle will vary by manufacturer. Our bundles contain approximately 200 strands each. To determine the number of bundles needed, divide the number of yarn strands needed by the number of strands in a bundle.

For example, if the Shopping List requires 3100 yarn strands, divide this by the number of yarn strands in a bundle to determine how many bundles are needed

3100 yarn strands divided by 200 (strands in a bundle) = 15.5. You will need 16 bundles.

Using Yarn from a Skein

If cutting your own strands from a skein, the number of yards per skein is listed on the yarn label. The label will also include a dye lot number. Be sure you have enough yarn of the same dye lot to complete the entire project.

To determine the total yardage needed, multiply the number of yarn strands needed (from the Shopping List) by the length of the yarn strands in a bundle (2½") to determine the total number of inches needed. Divide this number by 36" to get the total number of yards needed.

3100 x 2½" = 7750".

7750" divided by 36" = 215.3 yards

Cutting Your Own Yarn Strands

To cut your own strands, cut a 1¼" x 3" piece of cardboard. Wrap yarn around the cardboard along the shorter length from end to end ***(Fig. 3***; don't wrap too tight. Cover the length of the cardboard 3 times. Cut through the center of the cardboard ***(Fig. 4)*** to form yarn strands ***(Fig. 5)***. Count the number of strands made. Repeat this process until you have the approximate number of strands required.

Fig. 3

Fig. 4

Fig. 5

HOW TO LATCH HOOK

A gridded chart is given to indicate where yarn strands should be knotted to create the design. The color of each square on the chart indicates where on your gridded canvas to knot each color of yarn.

Using the color indicated on the chart, place your first knot 2" from the left side and bottom edges. To avoid errors, you may choose to mark 2" from the left side and bottom edges with permanent marker ***(Fig. 6)***.

Fig. 6

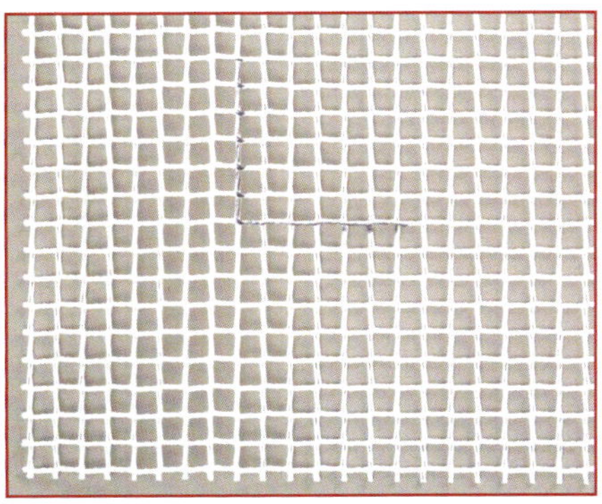

A latch hook tool consists of a metal shank with a handle. It is often bent to make it easy to use and easier on your hands. At the end of the shank is a hinged latch that helps create the knot. The latch should open and close easily.

1. Hold the latch hook tool in one hand. Loop a yarn strand around the tool, below the latch. Hold the yarn ends even with your other hand ***(Fig. 7)***.

Fig. 7

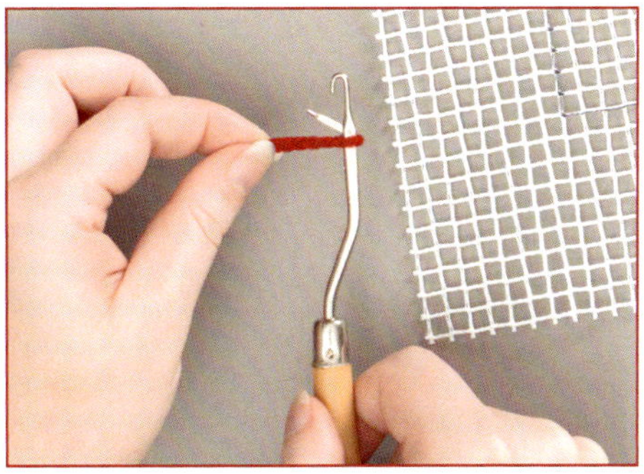

2. Insert the tool and open latch under one set of horizontal threads where you wish to make the knot ***(Fig. 8)***.

Fig. 8

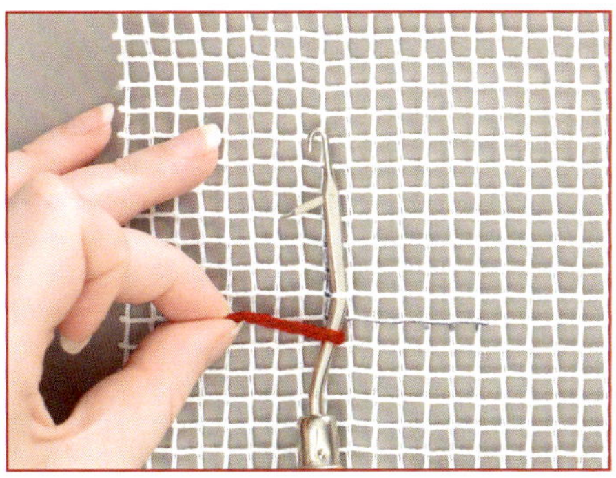

3. Place the yarn ends over the open latch ***(Fig. 9)***.

Fig. 9

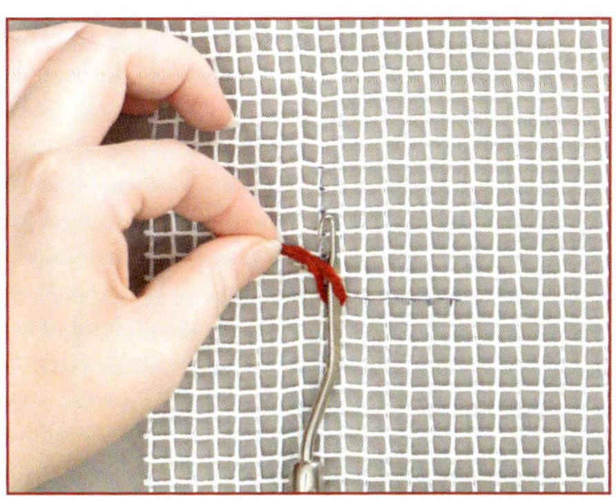

4. Slowly pull the tool back through the canvas so that the latch starts to close. As the latch closes, catch the yarn ***(Fig. 10)***. Wiggling the tool as you pull, turn the latch toward you and pull the yarn ends through the loop. Avoid letting the hook or latch catch the yarn strands.

Fig. 10

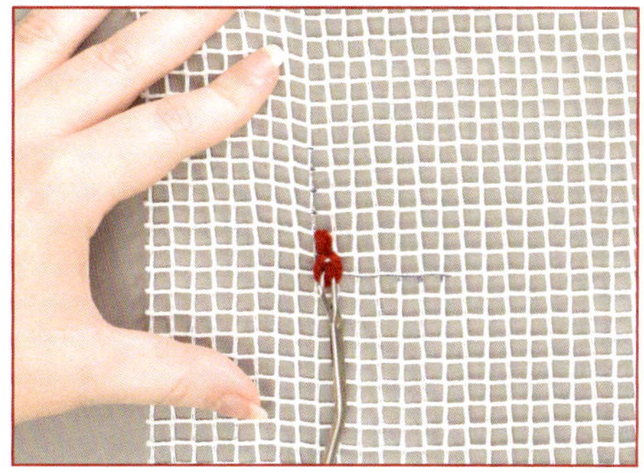

5. Holding the yarn ends even, pull the ends to tighten the knot ***(Fig. 11)***. If you make a mistake, pull the yarn out and try again.

Fig. 11

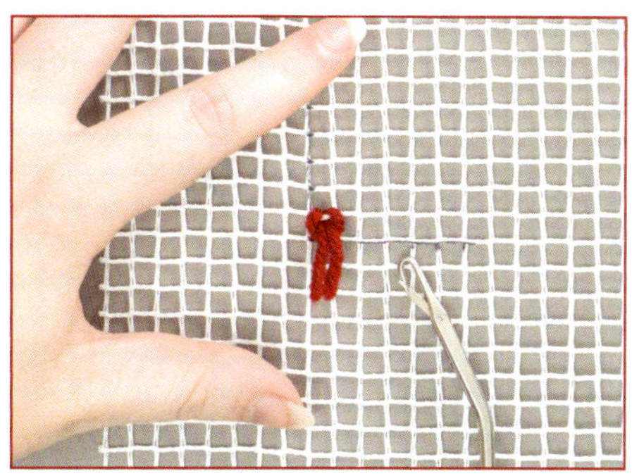

6. Work horizontally across the canvas, using the yarn color indicated on the chart. *(Fig. 12)*. Continue to work all rows.

Fig. 12

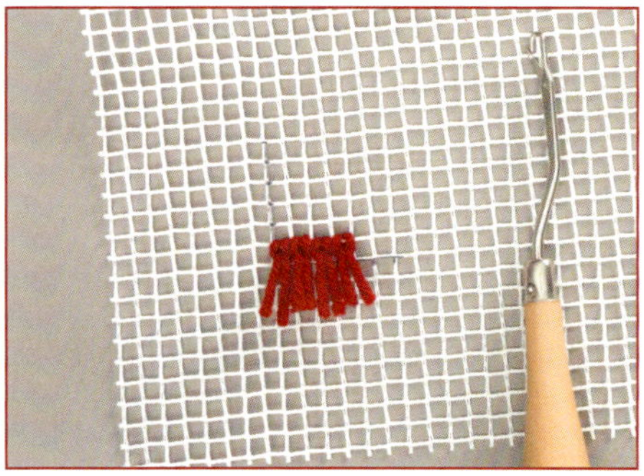

MAKING A WALL HANGING

1. Aligning the threads in the canvas, fold the excess canvas to the back along the thread closest to the knots. You may choose to use sewing clips or clothespins to hold the canvas in place. At each corner there will be an area of overlapping canvas that will be bulky. Cut out a square of canvas at each corner of your project *(Fig. 13)*

Fig. 13

2. Thread tapestry needle with a 36" length of yarn. Hand sew the edges to the back *(Fig. 14)*.

Fig. 14

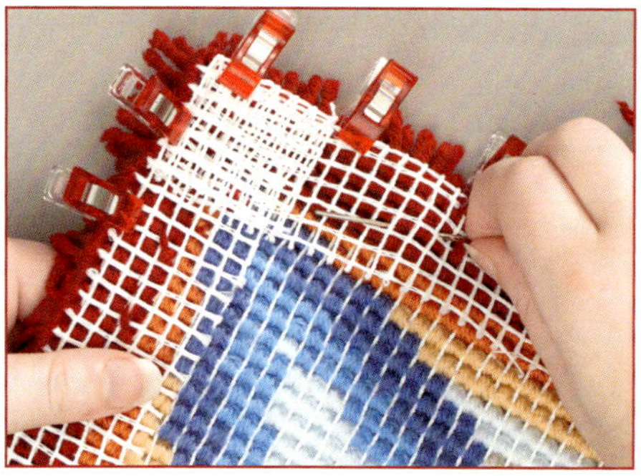

3. Use a Whipstitch to finish the edges. Thread a tapestry needle with a 36" length of yarn. Secure the tail of your working yarn with a knot. Bring the needle through each hole in the canvas 2-3 times to cover the canvas thread **(Fig. 15)**. Work around all edges of the wall hanging. Secure the yarn with a knot; trim.

Fig. 15

4. Glue the felt backing to your project and let dry completely.

TRIMMING

When you're finished with your latch hook project, trimming the yarn ends even will remove all the little imperfections and make for a beautiful finished project. If you didn't hold the yarn ends together perfectly or you snagged any yarns when knotting, trimming makes all your yarn strands more consistent in length. To trim the ends, run your fingers through the yarn strands to make the strands stand upright on your canvas. Delicately trim the rough ends. Don't get carried away with this. You can always trim more later. When you're finished, you may want to use a hand vacuum to clean up any fuzz.

HANGING YOUR WALL HANGING

Attach a few safety pins to the back along the upper edge to create hooks. Pin through the backing and a couple squares of the latch hook canvas ***(Fig. 16)***. Hang the safety pins on nails or wall hooks.

Fig. 16

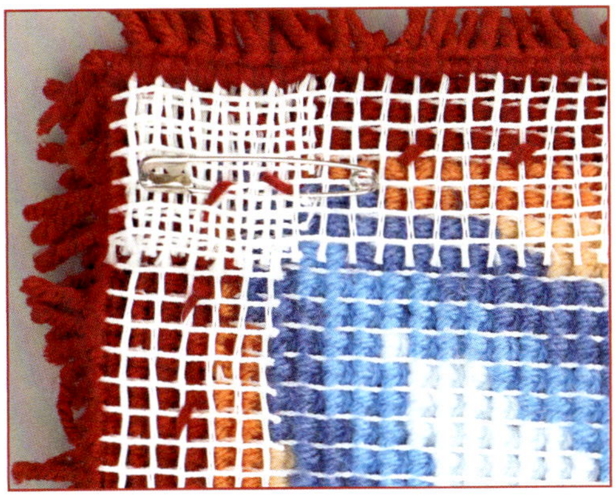

Show us what you're working on!

Share your project photos with us on social media.
Tag us @leisureartsinc or use #leisurearts

Images used under license from Shutterstock.com.

We have made every effort to ensure that these instructions are accurate and complete. We cannot, however, be responsible for human error, typographical mistakes, or variations in individual work.

Production Team: Technical Editor – Lisa Lancaster; Technical Associate Editor – Mary Sullivan Hutcheson; Senior Graphic Artist – Mark Hawkins; Photographer – Rob Karman

Special thanks to pattern testers Gary Hutcheson and Christopher Wright.

Made in U.S.A.